No One Sleeps Tonight

No One Sleeps Tonight

DAVID WEISS

TIGER BARK PRESS ✧ ROCHESTER, NEW YORK ✧ 2022

Published by Tiger Bark Press,
202 Mildorf Ave., Rochester, NY 14609.

Philip Memmer, Publisher.
Steven Huff, Founding Publisher.

Designed by Philip Memmer.

Cover art: *Large Myth #8* by Katherine Jackson.
Glass, RGB LED, steel. 15¼" x 11½" x 1".

ISBN-13: 979-8-9853587-2-8

Publication of this book was made possible by the New York State Council on the Arts with the support of the Office of the Governor and the New York State Legislature.

Contents

I

II

III

IV

In memory

of

CT & MW

Love the Greater has only so much patience
for the fearfulness of Love the Lesser

I

Don't be afraid, the clown's afraid too.

—Charles Mingus

A Sunlit Meadow

Sanity is a sunlit meadow across a valley you can only imagine

Sometimes it's a crow pecking out the eyes of a dead cat   strange as that
    may sound

Once it was your mother's boyfriend's son who felt the same way you did

In the high weeds deer lie down for what's left of the night

Crickets shake their can of coins

Is it sane or not   to soar with those sounds

Your mother stopped in that meadow and cracked open a milkweed pod

You watched her boyfriend watch her do this

In clumps the silk came out

You watched her watch some of it drift away

Tonight Arcturus like a tractor is baling the sky by orange torchlight

Crickets know something about unison that I don't

Sanity requires others   I know—although how many others I don't

Summer Solstice

A neurologic storm   this night-long fit of fire flies

The new moon   half a world away hidden in sunlight

In this deep dark the stars are our protesters   each holding up a placard of light

Bug and star   too quick or faint for the camera to catch

Gazing up from the grass   it's your breath that's naked

You can feel eyes you cannot see watching from the tree line

Stories have made the so-many stars into constellations   it would surprise them to know

You've left the windows open   coolness passes through without a sound

In the morning there'll be a molten sun   crows tagging the air

Once again you'll mistake seeing for being

Once again you'll hope for a beginning that won't make the old beginnings go silent

Until then you'll be like the new moon: entire   in transit   hard to pin down

Things I Can't Begin to Describe

When I was little
my father unscrewed his left arm from its socket
and hung a red dress in its place
a dress that drifted down from a Ferris wheel
Later my heart put that dress on

Who's to say the infant in tomorrow's arms
will know what to do with yesterday's paring knife
You wouldn't think you could cook fish cold in lemon juice
You wouldn't think you could be comfortable in your skin
Say it like you mean it   is not the same as meaning it

No Telling

There's no telling how long it will take the indigo bunting
to give up

In your experience you know you have to give up
over and over

The bird trills beneath the glass table-top
like hard candy sparkling in a cut-glass bowl

It flies up for a shiny thing that burst and made a child cry
It flies up again

Later will come flash flood warnings
that break in to interrupt the song on the radio

a song
you have long had by heart   as if you'd written it yourself

Yeah Right

1.

Too many blue-sky days in a row for hay to grow
—beneath springy alfalfa the ground's rock hard

Wild grape that's fastened on the young hackberry tree
is dragging it down like Madame Butterfly

I sever and disentangle the vines from it
as if unraveling the ties that bind

It too may not get back up
though in some versions   it does

2.

A friend of mine once bent
a six-inch nail in half with his hands
He did it so quietly
—bent over it   on his knees
applying unrelenting effort—
that when he stood and held it up
none of the Amish working with us
believed it for a minute
They were jokers too   practical jokers
Besides   they knew what belief was for

Aspirated Existence

To get from here   to the great creator world
is to shadow box inside a shadowbox

The language ladle hangs from a hook
to preside at the union of *once* and *will be*

which opens like a flower in the early Cretaceous
nothing if not seedy   nothing if not

becoming
nothing if not *nothing but*

Of Thee

for J. S.

The fundamentalist envies no one
The incestuous only what he can't imagine

The thought too awful to think
can't take its eyes off you

Inside the inside   wind is blowing
Grasses bend their seeded heads

For acts of God   only God may be sued
For acts of nature only nature

At a table in the commons room of the psych ward
Vladimir Lenin is trying to untangle Kurt Schwitters' "Cathedral of Erotic
    Misery"

Outside the outside   someone is weeping
You can see what troubles this trebuchet of mine

Live in the utopia of the dead body
That's what the hopeful say   dreaming of permission

Of   Of all words
the one I might relinquish last

What's left to love with?
Ask the girl

pumped from the ground
to irrigate the cotton fields of brother

It's a beautiful day
Liquid the song of the cardinal

In the utopia of knots what can be undone
that won't undo us?   Ask Lenin that one

It's a beautiful day   Anyone can see it's so
Just ask that girl   that sister

where all the prepositions start
Just ask her why she drinks so much

In the Bedroom

for D. S.

1. *Back Porch*

Rain (that unbroken all-day kind
which beat out on leaf and pavement alike
an unfluctuating, never-exactly-the-same
sidereal time) meant the world to me

and not monotony. Beneath the canvas awning
on the porch, I rocked and listened to
the drops that pinged the Rose of Sharon
and brimmed its blossoms' violet core.

From her bedroom window my grandmother
hummed her faraway song. The lacquered
girl with the watering can that hung on the fence,
showered the garden with wooden devotion.

2. *Gin Rummy*

The radio would play,
          the air conditioner hum.
Beside her useless legs I'd lie
          and deal the hand.

Outside, trade and traffic
          passed us by
like the indifferent, blazing sun.
          Heifetz fiddled

as we sloughed, laid off,
          angled for every point,
the score she tallied as densely
          numbered as ticker tape;

the stakes were high:
          for her, restlessness allayed;
and for me, boys evaded
          who prowled the alleys every day.

The total added up to
          little more than happiness,
the afternoon gone by.
          Men came home from work,

wives put the groceries away.
          Like a metronome she'd roll
her head from side to side, marking time
          when news not music would play.

3. *Containment*

In a scallop-edged tin coaster on
the bedside table her clear glass tumbler
stood night and day, a frosted helical
band incised just below the waterline.
Across the rim a paper doily lay.

Lesser silos around it,
her prescription bottles were arrayed:
warheads of prednizone, myocin, plaquinil,
marplex, catozim, percodan, trofamil,
darvon, mystedin, orange-muddy plastics

magnified by tap water. Their white caps
with *Star Drug* stamped in gold were
twisted off in sequence throughout her day.
Tepid, growing bubbly, the water sank
lower in the glass until things took on

their true proportions. My grandmother,
then, gave early warning, which went
unheeded in the din of the soap opera's
tremulous organ. As the world turned,
she cried from bed her ultimatums.

4. *Box*

Velveted, with rounded corners,
deeper than a deck of cards but
not much larger, elevated above
mirror glass on silvered balls:
put your eye to it, you could
see, reflected, that the bottom,
too, was burgundy, waled as
winter grass. A sprung-steel
hinge resisted opening
till open fully. I never heard her
ask to have it opened, never
peeked myself, but ran my finger-
tips along the pile, against
and with.

From it, up came an un-
domestic scent—no trace of illness in it
or velleity or eau de cologne
but of ermine wraps and opening night,
lipstick left on the cocktail's
rim, and a vapor of tonic-ed gin
which, wetting reddened lips,
ran back down without having
entered in.

It had no catch
or clasp. No frill or trim.
I'd lay my cheek beside it on
the glass, its secrets soundless,
sprung; I'd watch her wasting
in her bed, scarcely breathing,
the news and evening almost over,
but the night still falling and young.

5. *Intractable*

Chenille, too, the fringe
of the half-curtain which hung
down across the dressing
table where I hid, grottoed,

privy. There were groans in that room,
masking odors, skin
hanging in flaps, openings
more piteous than any I've

entered since. The bristles
of her bone-handled brush,
doubled in the mirror table
top, reached down and in

to prick the top of my head. I
sat crowned beneath the
rosy gums of her uppers
shipwrecked in glass; she

sat in traction, pulled on,
lengthening. Not a peep out
of either of us, straitened and
unstraightening, stretched to the limit.

6. *Wheelchair*

She'd be stood up,
maneuvered, set on the
cracked leather seat.
I would kneel before it, fold
the aluminum foot plates
down and place her shoed
misshapen feet on them, then
squire her out of the bedroom's
narrow cell and down
the hall. Stainless spokes
blurred along the worn
Persian runner which came
from Samarkand, she said.
That name made her think
of apricots in a bazaar,
heaped and orange, dried
to survive journeying.
I held the wide, rubber
grips, chest-high,
like a little horse in harness,
clip-clop. In the living room,
we stopped. Her head wobbled
like a white tulip in a bud vase,
which she steadied with a hand
that also needed steadying,
until all the figures
that lit our way winked
out. I kept my spot,
harness bells unshaking,
stalled in the damning
light of day.

7. *Bedpan*

Warm to the touch
its white enamel was,
after.

Lowered onto it,
levered off,
her hand, too,

that cupped my cheek
was soft,
unspeakably crooked.

Beneath the bed
it cooled, went cold
beneath newsprint.

The fat-bellied, never-not-laughing Buddha
cradled a cone of incense
in its smoking lap.

Long after,
it would lie on the closet floor,
untouched.

Autumn Equinox

Right behind you   at eye level
the sun   that same old
that oxidizer   that hypnotic yolk
going down   turning
the hillside to coals

It's everything you're not
—amen to that
though once   *once*
you were almost no one enough
almost that untouchable

Now the sun drops into its slot
and it's done   like a drug wearing off
love and its G force   done
this elegiac glow   which comes
as if out of each and every thing   done

And now   the dusky borders
are opening   unpoliced
all of us made equals   all of us made shadows
and then   just a single sunless shadow
that has its own politics

Winter's Winter

The sun is no one's father
The moon just a need to see in the dark

Not a needle on the pines is EKGing
but you can't tell me they're not busy

with their own machinations   They forged
their alliances   long since

A locket of ice encases the cosmos
those late, self-trellising flowers

Only to us is waiting *waiting*
The sun   that orphan   that Decembrist

won't rise above the tree tops today
Hardly vivant this tableau

When the black locust falls it shatters like a chandelier
Only later will the sky be brighter for it

You can never die before your time
it hurts to say

Human relations are too much
No wonder indifference is such a relief

the indifference we call ecology
the indifference we call necessity

as if to say   come out   the game is over
And yet we feel most free to act

when things are out of our hands
O beloved space between every last little thing

in your quietude we hear it   the *making-*
it-up-as-we-go   pounding in our ears

The tree lies on its side   one of its many sides
Snow will have to find its own way

back into the sky   The dark will have to
feel its way in the dark   What's the sun

worth an hour for making us happy
what's the moon for making us visible

Come As You Are

And when it happens
        more vivid than required by law
she need never know another night is coming

Soul's the thing beyond expression
        spellbound and binding
like mangrove roots fishes flit among

She loves what's near to us   the far off she also loves
        She turns to see who it is coming toward her
as evening does from across the water

Evening   more vivid than law itself
        burning the eastern hills orange
Tonight   let information weep for a change

II

We are never so far off that it is no more to be heard

—E.M. Remarque

Impart

If I can think of it, it isn't what I want.
— Randall Jarrell

Why I've lived and you haven't isn't clear to me
except that

my clock stopped long ago and yours tells
the date and time

The second amendment should never have been
placed so close to the first

For the life of me I don't know why you've lived
and I haven't . . .

Laws we haven't made hold sway
words we haven't said stand guard

From the smithy of the bone marrow
hymns blow like flies

The past imparts itself like a school-yard chant
you've known all along

To the screen door comes *harm*   that child
who got lost on her way home

and now there will be no going home
How can your heart not go out to her

What It Means to Undress

She cannot zip her dress all the way up in back
without some help

Nor can she undo the clasp
or zip the dress down by herself

What you know of her now amounts
to counting back from Armageddon

The whisper of insect legs is like crumbs
the baker makes   slicing bread

Eternity   that fermata   comes in thimblefuls
A grain of sand has its own way to swallow the sea

If she doesn't come back tonight
that owl flying into the sun

will be her   at last

No One Sleeps Tonight

To have been born   is to
take notice   of sunlight dressed as moonlight
of a girl on a swing   is to

take down from the mantle
the cherub that trumpets   and turns
as it plays   in moonlight dressed as sunlight

is to correct for enchantment   for smallness   for illness
as she listens in the high-backed armchair
to *Nessun Dorma* on the Victrola

To be the leather belt hooked inside her closet door
to be the brocade curtains hanging almost to the floor
and to watch her listen   cheek in hand   is to listen

to your being there

A Wave of Her Hand

Without a wave of her hand   she was gone
The morning with its discount rate didn't come   didn't come
Outside the window   a *cordon sanitaire* was set up

to incubate the future
Decisions are no easier for not being decisions
Was it this that she was not waving to

What Good

What good will it do now   songstress
What timber won't burn   what man won't go
Even marble columns are made of smoke

When you sing   a pitched battle
takes place between notes
and melody   that orphan   swoops down from its branch

There's reverie inside the hailstone
To take into account   and   *to account for*
are as alike as sweet uproar can make us

Figura

There is such voodoo in the uncomforted mind

I was wakened this morning by her unfading affliction

Once a body could have been placed on a horse without suspicion

What finds us   comes as doctrine   or comes mizzling and soft
    like a hallway with no doors in it

Face that I know so close up   so well

with its high towers   with its meadow ringed by trees

What happens when obligation has nothing left to do

A Matter Of

That was the day the foundries fell quiet
The propositions let A and B go   to start their own dynasties

That was the day the planetary green stood in full regalia
like an armistice beneath the interned air

Wildfires of icebound morning burned the homestead down
to a palindrome of medicine and milk

A day like any other day   like a moment hidden
inside the day that persists in its play

It carries an efflorescence down
into the rising waters

The Committee of the Whole

We were bitter united and sang an In Nomine
that ran the gamut from P53 to Dear John
as though *never mind* meant *mindful of*
as though accidents were systematic
and the wheel were a wind instrument

We shared an understanding of *up a creek without* and *do the math*
We took all we knew about the wilderness
and all we knew about embarrassment
and ran them through the secret language of
the experience we call *the experience of others*

Someone is counting
Someone is struggling
Someone is mapping her pillow
Someone is pulverizing *not so simple*   to fill the hourglass
Someone is on the far side of *in-between*
Someone is   and then someone else is   and heaving into view is
    yet another someone

There is a factory somewhere in tarnation
that makes one item   one unit   one thing   at a time
and that one thing is no *thing* at all

Truancy Among the Centuries

There was the roadblock taste of love a headwind
reek of blood a push that sounds like shove

In the end the cervix was hoarse from shouting
the pronouns covered in bruises

But she was attributed ushered into that revealed estate
where the primrose is grafted onto the permanence of cooling

And if it's true that the end itself will be deforested
and that rising water will cover over the cacophonies

you will still hear the excited sounds of children
lining the parade route

The Hind Legs Are Ancestral

How she kissed him   hectares of spirit cannot express
An equilateral triangle shall escort the hypotenuse to the altar

Our past histories are unreprintable   in quarantine
Yet-to-be crosses the X spot like knowing mournful Demeter

Habañeros of intimacy undulate like a caterpillar
There's a fire in the needlework   you can be sure of that

Like no tomorrow is how tomorrow teaches us to think
as it drills a hole in the carrot   for the stick

A Dozen of Roses

jetting up   blooding the eye

A Dozen of Roses   immigrant eloquent
creams and crimsons   tightly scrolled   manifold

In sidewalk cracks: grass
that tireless biographer of grass

In dumpsters: rats
those busy archivists of *rattus rattus*

And a *Dozen of Roses?*
So like us   shoulder to shoulder   not fully open

Something must be *so*
beyond this shelf life   beyond this reckoning

A Dozen of Roses! I'm in love
with them   my personal saviors!   as I am with you

Anything to make you laugh
and throw off fate like lantern light

like a blanket
sweated through at night

Night the historiographer of night
of getting through it

True is what's tried   what
we're left to say it with

What isn't inadequate?
We're stopped   standing at the light

where north pools into east
west into south

We haven't yet but we're about
to step off the curb   that precipice

into the motley teeming mix
the dozens of   carried along   like a beacon

just as any rubber-banded bouquet of roses
      taken in hand   must be

The Rule of Slide

The agony cache lies buried   like a music box   under the practicable

But you already know that

You already know we must get beyond the exclamation points   above
the cry line

Our job is to go inquiring   as others have gone a-maying

If you'll be *for*   I'll be *of*   we can climb inside of *with* together

As if out to sea we have been swept along by lab results   the agora   by
dissident clay

Would it help if the harrow were less restless   the thunderhead less
magnificent

We'll have to count on the grammar of doxology to achieve escape velocity

The Room

for CT

It was nothing to speak of
that empty room
the mattress on the floor
pushed up against the radiator
a window so dirty the streetlamp cast no shadows
a bathroom at the end of the hall
She lay undressed in a motheaten fur coat
I lay beside her
She wrapped us in it

It was a moment even the words to describe it
couldn't describe
The great domesticating enterprise left its arts at the door
The picture on the wall was only an outline of where a picture had once hung
Someone had lived here
Someone will always have lived here
All we had in that cold room was our being there
All we had was wanting nothing else
and the making it all up that went with it

Blessing

It all happened so quickly:
what I said, his fist,
my sprawling, his drunken kicks,
the bartender gripping my face
in his huge hand once I
struggled to my feet.
Yet
it took forever, it seemed,
like the irreversible lifetime
between slammed-on brakes
and impact. For years I recalled
only the figure I cut
as I shrieked, flat on my back,
and later groped along
the floor for my glasses.
I see
now how overdressed
for that bar she was
in her peasant skirt, richly
embroidered, the black leotard top,
the turquoise necklace.
This was
a bar where the drinking
was serious and steady, the silence
behind the backbeat sullen,
stiff with craving. More
of her then unscarred body
comes into view,
a girl's really, unfinished,
all I knew.

I hadn’t noticed
him then, but I do now—gaunt,
tattooed, with hard blue eyes,
a Vet, recently returned,
bellied-up, putting back
bourbons before lurching over.

Who in hell do you think
you are coming in here
dressed like that, tits
sticking out, mocking us.
Someone ought to teach you
a lesson, girlie. And me, approaching,
the lady doesn’t want to be
bothered, can't you see that, friend?
a line right out of the movies.
Right before
I went reeling across the floor,
though, was a moment I owe
to his hurt, vengeful eyes.
Stepping between them I forgot
where I was, caught in the thrilling
scent of perfume and sweat,
the flush of her throat,
just as he must have been too.
It stunned me.
All I’d wished for until then
had been beyond reach,
unattainably elevated and glorious,
that pure curse of adolescence
which goes wry or bitter in us.
My God, I thought, she’s *mine*

and meant: I am crossing over.
It stretched away before me
like the land of milk and honey.
When he turned me toward him
I had no idea why.
I didn't feel
that first punch; his fist kissed
my chin like a blessing, stamping
the instant indelibly with his vision
of it as well—it was this:

love is something I'll never have.
Months later her death was
another punch.
She died on route,
narrowing the distance between us,
a collision so powerful
it snapped her heart off
its stem and disfigured her terribly;
they sealed the coffin
shut.
No distance between us
I can take her
into more than my arms
wishing still for that life
which no one could grant us—
not ourselves then,
not myself now.
And yet,
it's more than a daydream,
more even than a memory:
I let her take my hand,

I let her lead me out.
I can be the fool now
I could never let myself be.
I can give myself up
to her greater envisionings.

That

For MW

she should die and I . . .

That she should die and stone
win its long cooling argument with sun

That she should die and one final tear
leak from her finally closing eye

and bile blackly green and thick
ooze from her parted lips

That she should die to leave us sift
through all she may have been

That she should die and laughter laugh
without her laugh to laugh along

That she should die and I keep
talking to her and she to me

as though maternity could live
beyond even the wish for it

That she should die and sun
lose its long hot argument with stone

is only fair and sad and so
But mostly so and sad and fair

and so
that she should die

III

What we've made is clear
what we make of it is not

Insolvency

A failed state is one that goes on failing
Outcomes angle down   like incomings

They tear holes in the map of
business as usual

Behind the ears a sweet darkness
Grapes cluster on the outskirts

Thus Marcus Aurelius paused in his labors
and gazed out through the tent flaps

Typeface has taken the place of evidence
To refuse is best to do in ballad form

Anyone who is anyone
is working on the problem of a more perfect reunion

Crickets pulse with a single wish
It's too bad we won't be there for it

Minutiae is inoperable
In the meantime just ask a preschooler if hollering is an *a capella* thing

Anyone who is anyone will lead us straight under the mountain
The rest of us put our faces into the wind

The undersigned affirms that the aforesaid
is true to the best of his knowledge

The Regency Period

To be outside the outside   and no sugarcoating it

To be inside the inside   that unmedicated embrace

How unexpected that wooing should increase our strangeness

You cannot plead with a pond

You cannot bleach out the warlord dyes

Yet a hundredfold can still be unfolded

A ferry can be ferried and still be a ferry

We live as though a white tablecloth   and all the place settings
    have been laid in the crosswalk

They Make Lament on the Strange Trees

—Canto XIII, Inferno

the soil ashen beneath their human beaks
Once they made sure it was not okay

Furious they dove into the mind and made
refuge alien

Now they must count on decency coupling
with the indecent to keep the monstrous grunting   occupied

Burnt-out as stars   rage-depleted
they loll on branches like feathered chili peppers

If they could they would roll the sun back down to cockcrow
until the bread trucks are loading their loaves again

until men are snoring in their beds   throats uncut
their children not yet sweet in their mouths

They would winch midnight back to twilight
before father and daughter have turned out the lights

Once when the mind moved in its aviary
like kingfisher or shag

the great transgressions were a turbulent Aegean to dive through
the laws of succession as clear as spinal fluid

You can see how they're spent: talons blunted   neuropathic
consigned to mythology

It takes a group effort now to do the sort of harm
that petrifies the heart and turns the mind white

Listen to them whetting their squawk
They know we're still theirs once the caissons start rolling

We wheel in thrilled unison above their heads
like orphans   like shrapnel

Far Off   Described

. . . as the songs of birds in the woods
— Kierkegaard, *Fear and Trembling*

You can still make them out against the dry hills
rocking on their camels   the days ahead
designed to make the edict simmer on the coals
of *can't* and *must*   *Far off* forms in the eye's mind
unravels the belonging that keeps them warm
Too much attention has been paid to the knife
Not enough to the beauty of obedience
Not enough to the terror of obedience
Obedience   far off at the end of words   beyond assurance
Nothing is worse than to make another one's instrument
Nothing worse than to submit without belief
Without a covenant how could they ever trust each other
The ram is the story they make up—who could understand it otherwise
the ram they came on in a thorn bush   and slaughtered
its life their evidence   its horns their reenactment

Out of thin air they return as if growing larger not nearer
Far off   that invisibility
of having lain in each other's arms against the cold
Locusts rub the air raw
as though nature were applauding these two dusty now life-sized males
No one sees the spark that ignites the greater darkness
that blueprint for how the voluntary and involuntary can't be told apart
that crypt of what men will do without women

Where Judgment Stops

for H.S.

To plot a triangle and to concentrate all force at the apex
is to mistake *What should I do?*
for *What have I done?*

To hear Sophocles tell it
you'd think suffering was the price
for turning grief into a story

As Thucydides tells it   no depravity is uncivil
Place the beloved in one pan   the rock of ages in the other
and you can mistake equilibrium for equivalence

As Apollo sees it
breast cancer lights up the northeast
HIV makes the earth glitter from outer space

"I mean, what's money after all?"
Dombey's motherless son asks his father
intuiting what exchange is really for

Come in low over the tree tops
and you'll come upon *I just can't!* weeping
in front of *Somebody has to do it!*

To hear Proust tell it
we live in the body of the broken heart
sweeping up   sweeping up

And when judgment lays out its arguments
like bright surgical instruments
remember that it will still take off its robes

for the chance to hook a gold ring
as if grabbing hold of something
it had lost

Not To

She did not merely exercise a great influence
Between one breath and another Madame S.
vanished in the twilight   music under her arm
Her touch made custard foam from the database

She did not merely acquaint single parents with the zoösphere
She had the gift of candle flame   of defibrillating it
She evangelized the body politic with her own form of happiness
even as infants lay in the earth of our metallurgical times

She taught us to   and she taught us not to
and how a marble floor may be bordered by peonies
Maggots will seethe in the cinders   and utmost kindness too
Summer   a summer's eve   she vanished

as warm asphalt without flinching gazed up at the stars
She'd held an inchworm in the palm of her hand
plus a wry willingness . . .
and let's not forget the row of tiny mother-of-pearl buttons

Theodicy of Matchsticks

Ova the Logician   hard at work on her loom   will tell you:
mitosis has solved the problem of loss
just as tapestry solves the problem of politics

Any river you think uncrossable will have the old chill   the stone-song
persistent as a tea rose holding its note late into the season
The up-against-it know something about reconfiguring sunshine

The years won't leave a sound behind
Seconds   linchpin heavy   drift like snow
But everything to come retains a trace of us

the way the sky looks down on us
through the branches of trees in winter

Proprioceptive

Before head and heart   we stood
as if before the town clerk and her daughter
the one wearing water wings
whose thrill-splashed shrieks free-climbed the upper octaves

Life's an interruption—an uninterrupted one
Someone's always afraid of a licking
In the tumulus of the genitals a wail goes up
Night a flag you can unwrap yourself in

From birdsong   kenosis takes flight
What you reach out and touch
will not engulf thee   The coordinates
are ours   but the velocity isn't

IV

It's what I've never seen that I recognize.

—Diane Arbus

Nobody Likes to Come Back to Life

because . . . what for?
There are a lot of reasons   I know
but it's only the living who think they're good ones

Gone   reasons go too
Once   yes   you were like everyone else
and also like no one else

But   for the quick
who still have some choice in the matter
it matters

when there's a difference to be made
—many small irrefutable
differences   really

that will be measured at last in tears
and marked by ceremonies of voice and fire
The space that closes up

seamlessly   like a magic trick
around those who are gone
doesn't close fast

For the observant   aka the grieving
the seamless is scarred
as a lake is   when a stone falls into it

the ring of water   widening
toward the distant bank   dwindles
but it gets there

Best might be to live on both sides at once
the way the word *then*
refers to what's past   and to what's next

like an image in a mirror   and the mirror itself
Or like an image in a mirror   and the image maker
who isn't making images any longer

although still making mirrors

Version Two

Before the house of changes
    the guard dogs lie down among the downhearted

Another way of saying this is: expectation is a kind of house arrest
    Belief is rich in butterfat

Who among us isn't a flycatcher among owls
    an infinitive among stones

What   even among yellow wax beans mounded high
    is without interiority

Childhood question #17:
    how do minds *meet*   and where

I will bear in mind that even a nosedive
    must take the plunge

And a kiss: is it hook   line
    or sinker

Winter sunlight through the bedroom window
    With it comes the feeling sometimes

that one has settled for too much.

Taking To It (Scat Song for a New Born)

for Isidore

All lines of sight in the Einsteinian universe
lead back to the beginning. Our birth surrounds us.
— Dennis Overbye

Come out   you
and be born
be a fact
keep time
like the carpenter bee
whose atomic
clock is lighter than
air
Come out   you
secreting secrets
clandestine at first
then a clan
Fling   that first motion
of flap
lifts the caddisfly
and green lacewing
into precedented air
Here in this
ninety-odd
millionth spring
wherever you'll turn
all moving away
is toward
the origin of
moving away   So
come out
be new in
minute detail
and pat the patterns—

there's a dog *Mythos*
good boy *Helix*
that's it *Helios* *Up!—*
faithful mutts
which have tricks
to play
none to learn
Come out you
and face the music
its insect symphonium
dandelion-muted
like Roy Eldritch
on trumpet no
sound quite
like it
Come out you
it's your fate to
poor thing
Take your sweet time
hover in slow
flight gather
sip at the knee of
before it takes you
for a ride
with the top down
wind a singing
rush *was* rhyming
is *doing*
being and all
you can do then
is catch
the rhythm of
fan-like throw-off

and   little baby
great nay-saying
sport of nature
scat

Our Eyes Are Dry   Child

for K. J.

No one is worried about you   distant star
No one's worried   seedling

In the temple of close proximity
you can be mad as you want

On the Broadway stage of the cosmos
no one is paying attention

Unison: a form of drowning out

Whoever worries about you is also living your life
Your life: whatever you can't keep from happening

You have to assent to something
Let it be each beloved word that asks nothing of you

and pours like sunlight through leaded glass

Teased

Late afternoon sunlight   migrating
its rectangle across the wall

To be so disarmed
by this shadow puppetry of branch and leaf and breeze

with no story to tell   beyond
that of shimmer and shift and happenstance

Amid the bad news of cancer uncontained
of a daughter's vicissitudes   car bombs   a bunged knuckle

I've gone up to it   to get close to this living brushwork
only to make it disappear

When I draw back   it resumes its play
of glimmery unintention   self-creating   without a care

I can only put down my pen
before what will leave no trace

attendant on   yet not anxious about
the evening coming on

Illumined

for L. E.

Small night celebrates the great night
I copied this out like a scribe of the monastery at Salzburg
Later I paged back to find the poem and that line
It was missing like the eldest son of a brutal father
I reread that entire book of Serbian poetry
Clues abounded—every other word was *night*
I took the line for my own like a berry in the beak of a gliding bird
Small night (that's us) *celebrates the great night*
(you know what that is)
It's hard to celebrate without a tear in your eye
The great in this way is carried in the arms of the small
a codex in a croker sack copied in majuscule
or minuscule in the gale-force medieval dark   by candlelight
Great night will be spoken for
In gilded script   *small night*   its squire
setting down its own stars   leads the way

The Man I'll Never Be

for WZK

Any sign you receive, for good or ill,
you must first tell to the mountains.
—Ismail Kadare

It is good that a knife is sharp
and a bowl is curved,
that water seeks its level
and luck is undeserved.

It is good to be a father,
and good to be a son,
good to step out of doors
naked to the waist and the sun.

It is good to lay block, to cinch
a rope, good to frame
a house and an argument,
to say the beloved name.

It is good to drive a nail,
good how a screw pulls in.
When it's set, mortar won't soften.
Set, the mind's hard, certain.

That bread rises and evening falls,
that water boils and crows caw,
that you are master within arm's length
and servant of the unwritten laws

is good, just as to stake the boundaries
or snap off a broken twig
is, or to run your hand along her spine,
or to take up a shovel and dig.

It is good to love, good also
to hate, to return a look
and repay a debt—to plunge
your face in the fire of an icy brook.

It is good to raise a song,
songs are a kind of wheel,
good that we feel what it says,
that it says what we feel.

It is good to dandle an infant—
that cleanly smell, the absorbing eye—
good not to know who shall live
and when it is you'll die.

To stand and speak is good,
good, too, to be heard,
good to sit in judgment,
to wield a final word.

More is better than less,
except for trouble and talk.
Enough is best: eat your fill
and toss the bottle off.

It's best to be alive, to crack
a walnut in your fist, next
to take a last look, then to go.
To own nothing. Nothing to owe.

Acknowledgments

Hole in the Head Review:

"Blessing"

"Things I Can't Begin to Describe"

"The Committee of the Whole"

About the Author

David Weiss has published five previous collections of poems: *The Fourth Part of the World* (Ohio State University Press), *Gnomon* (Wolf at the Door Press), *Perfect Crime* (Nine Mile Books), *Per Diem* (Tiger Bark Press), *Little Mirror* (Lynx House Press), and one novel, *The Mensch.* His essays, translations, and poems have appeared over the years in *The Atlantic, Parnassus, The New Yorker, Iowa Review, North American Review, Modern Poetry in Translation, Crazyhorse, Ploughshares* and *Hole in the Head Review,* among others. He edited *Seneca Review* for many years and taught at Hobart and William Smith Colleges.

More Poetry from Tiger Bark Press

When I Was Water, by Deena Linett
World Happiness Index, by Kathleen Aguero
Hard Work in Low Places, by Stephen Lewandowski
The Foreigner's Song, by Pablo Medina
Old Horse, What Is to Be Done? by Stephen Kuusisto
The Half-Life, by Roger Greenwald
Psychometry, by Georgia A. Popoff
I Play His Red Guitar, by Charles Coté
Per Diem, by David Weiss
Boy on a Doorstep, by Richard Foerster
Totem: America, by Debra Kang Dean
After Morning Rain, by Sam Hamill
Meditation Archipelago, by Tony Leuzzi
Fancy's Orphan, by George Drew
Translucent When Fired, by Deena Linett
Ask Again Later, by Nancy White
Pricking, by Jessica Cuello
Dinner with Emerson, by Wendy Mnookin
As Long As We Are Not Alone, by Israel Emiot,
translated by Leah Zazulyer
Be Quiet, by Kuno Raeber, translated by Stuart Friebert
Psalter, by Georgia Popoff
Slow Mountain Train, by Roger Greenwald
The Burning Door, by Tony Leuzzi
I've Come This Far to Say Hello: Poems Selected and New, by Kurt Brown
After That, by Kathleen Aguero
Crossing the Yellow River, translated by Sam Hamill
Night Garden, by Judith Harris
Time-Bound, by Kurt Brown
Sweet Weight, by Kate Lynn Hibbard
The Gate at Visby, by Deena Linett
River of Glass, by Ann McGovern
Inside Such Darkness, by Virginia Slachman
Transfiguration Begins at Home, by Estha Weiner
The Solvay Process, by Martin Walls
A Pilgrim into Silence, by Karen Swenson